Leslie —
Palisades

A SEARCH FOR THE
PERFECT DOG

A SEARCH FOR THE PERFECT DOG

GARY SHIEBLER

BROADWAY BOOKS   NEW YORK

BROADWAY

A SEARCH FOR THE PERFECT DOG. Copyright © 1997 by Gary
Shiebler. All rights reserved. Printed in the United States of
America. No part of this book may be reproduced or transmitted in
any form or by any means, electronic or mechanical, including
photocopying, recording, or by any information storage and
retrieval system, without written permission from the publisher. For
information address Broadway Books, a division of
Bantam Doubleday Dell Publishing Group, Inc.,
1540 Broadway, New York, NY 10036.

Broadway Books titles may be purchased for business or promotional
use or for special sales. For information, please write to: Special
Markets Department, Bantam Doubleday Dell Publishing Group,
Inc., 1540 Broadway, New York, NY 10036.

BROADWAY BOOKS and its logo, a letter B bisected on
the diagonal, are trademarks of Broadway Books, a division of
Bantam Doubleday Dell Publishing Group, Inc.

Library of Congress Cataloging-in-Publication Data

Shiebler, Gary.
A search for the perfect dog / Gary Shiebler. — 1st ed.
p.   cm.
ISBN 0-7679-0026-X
1. Dogs—United States—Anecdotes. 2. Shiebler, Gary. I. Title.
SF426.2.S54   1997
636.7'0092—dc21   97-16350
[B]   CIP

FIRST EDITION

Designed by Ellen Cipriano

Photo credits: p. xv © Ellsworth Shiebler; p. 25, 31, 103 © Gary
Shiebler; pp. 39, 49, 77, 111 © Linda Holmstrom

97 98 99 00 10 9 8 7 6 5 4 3 2 1

CONTENTS

....

ACKNOWLEDGMENTS

....

FOR MANY YEARS I BELIEVED THAT I HAD TO DO EVERYTHING alone. The following people proved to me that reaching out and asking for help is not a sign of weakness but a sign of strength. Their love and support touch every page in this book.

I thank my wife, Linda, for her endless patience and faith, for all the sacrifices she has made, and for sticking around long enough to see the fruits of my dreams.

I thank my daughter, Hayden. There have been no greater joys in my life than the ones that have come from being her father.

I thank my parents for always believing in me.

I thank my brother, Glenn, and sister, Susan, for their continuing love and support.

I thank my agent, Rhonda Winchell, who called me one Sunday morning while I was making scrambled eggs to tell me how much she loved the book. I am very grateful to her for all her hard work and dedication.

I thank my editor, Charles Conrad, whose gentle guiding hand steered this book to where I ultimately wanted it to be.

I thank Sally Jaskold for smoothing the rough edges and for her caring and respectful input.

I thank my dear friend, writer Dawn Hayes O'Leary, who was never too busy to listen to me wail or hear a rewrite over the phone. I could not have finished this book without her.

I thank Geoff Willis, who gave me the courage to believe that I could write this book.

I thank the adoptions staff at the Helen Woodward Animal Center, particularly J. J. and Jodie. Their love and commitment to the dogs will forever be an inspiration to me.

Lastly, I thank all the dogs that have blessed my life.

A SEARCH FOR THE PERFECT DOG

INTRODUCTION

....

A FEW YEARS AGO I WAS STANDING ON A BLUFF OVERLOOK-
ing the Pacific Ocean. A warm wind was blowing from
the east and it gently feathered the waves as they broke
on the shore below. Seagulls frolicked in the updrafts
along the cliffs, and a school of porpoises swam joyfully
just beyond the breakers. The air was fresh and salty clean
and the morning sun bathed my back with its early light.

It was a perfect day.

I remember thinking, "Gary, if you can't find happiness in this moment, you're in big trouble."

I was in big trouble.

I took off my cap and sat down. I had dreamed
about this moment for many years but I was afraid to step

into it. And as I sat above that magnificent scene, I realized that, for much of my life, I had been searching for something that didn't exist. The perfect place to live. The perfect job. The perfect marriage. The perfect family.

The perfect life.

A few days later, just a couple miles from the cliffs where I stood that Monday morning, I accepted a job that would change the course of my life. I would meet many of the brave and honorable spirits that fill the pages of this book. My search for perfection would end and I would rediscover the joys and delights of the simple and ordinary things of life. I would begin to forgive myself for all the things I hadn't achieved, the goals I hadn't reached, and the mistakes I had made. Here I would be inspired by the unwavering faith and spirit of Champ, the devotion and dignity of Chaz and Sunshine, and the quiet acceptance and courage of Patches. I would even learn to accept and embrace the endearing flaws and imperfections of a very special dog named Canyon.

These noble and heroic animals have helped me to tame the restlessness and confusion of my middle years and softened the sorrows and bewilderments of growing older in a world that seems to be only growing younger. I have learned that when I begin to feel overwhelmed by the world around me, I can turn away from the inanimate things that so easily influence my life—the televisions, the radios, the newspapers, the computers—and return to the living things. For here I will find the peace I seek, the contentment I long for, the perfection I so desperately desire.

For some, this kind of peace may come from digging in the garden, walking along a vibrant shoreline, or rising and falling above the gallop of a horse. For me, it has always come from having a dog by my side. Often disguised by their simplicity and grace, these living things are all around us, all too willing to help us on our journeys. And in a time when so many of us have lost faith in our fellowman, perhaps it will be these living things that will create a bridge, a safe crossing to a place of compassion, tolerance, and understanding of our own kind. For me and countless others, dogs will always be a sanctuary, a safe harbor. A place to go when the world seems too big, the demands too great, and the rewards too small.

I will forever be grateful for the gifts, comfort, and love they have so freely given me.

I am a lucky man.

When I think of the profound relationships between people and dogs and of the legacy a dog can leave with a man, I have to go back to the very beginning.

To a dog named Rusty.

"WE BE OF ONE BLOOD, THOU AND I."

—RUDYARD KIPLING

RUSTY

....

WHEN I WAS A BOY, I WAS CONVINCED THAT A ghost lived in my bedroom closet. My parents had renovated the attic of our brown-shingled Dutch Colonial and turned it into two bedrooms—one for me and one for my younger brother. My brother's room was on the sunny south side of the house. It was a simple, boxy room with a couple windows and a small closet. My bedroom, on the north side, had spooky nooks, landings, and crawl spaces, sharp-angled ceilings that dipped to darkened corners, two tiny windows, and this massive closet. Almost every night before I went to sleep, the closet door would have to be closed.

On some brave nights, I would decide to leave the

door open a crack. I would brazenly turn off the light, pull the covers up, and close my eyes.

I'd call to my brother in the next room, "Glenn?"

No answer. He always fell asleep before I did.

Then a rogue creak or mysterious thump would spring my eyes open and set my pulse racing. I would peek over the covers and watch the door like a hawk. The hall light would begin to play tricks with my wide eyes and tender imagination. The small crack of pitch black would begin to grow. The gold doorknob would slowly begin to turn and the tips of ghoulish fingers would appear, curling around the door frame.

"Daaadd! Come close the closet door!" I'd yell.

My dad would bound up the stairs, three steps at a time, and close the door for me. He would assure me that the ghost was not strong enough to open the door by himself. I don't think he ever tried to convince me the ghost wasn't there. He'd just always come to the rescue.

One Tuesday morning when I was three years old, a very thin, baked-potato-brown dog appeared outside our front door.

"I opened the door and he was just standing there," my mother remembers. "He was an absolute mess. I called your father at work and he immediately came home and took him up to Dr. Barry's. It turned out that he had one of the worst cases of mange he had ever seen. Dr. Barry didn't think he was going to make it. 'I'll try my best to save him,' he told me. 'But it's very serious.' In those days, the only way they treated such severe cases of mange was with arsenic.

"It was a miracle that he recovered," she recalled. "Slowly he regained his strength. And all those bare patches of skin and brown mats of fur were soon replaced with as glorious an orange coat as I had ever seen."

We named him Rusty.

He would become the dog against which I would measure all others.

To this day, my mom says there will never be another dog like him. And though my memories of him are fuzzy and gilded by a simpler and more innocent time, an imprint on my heart says it is so.

With the passing of years, I have forgotten many of the details about Rusty. Most have dissolved into myth or are bound by stories shared at dinner tables and in holiday living rooms.

I look at old photographs.

I see a dog sitting beside me on a braided rug in front of a small Christmas tree.

I want to remember the touch of his fur.

I see a young boy sitting proudly on a blue bicycle with a dog standing beside him.

I want to remember the sound of his bark.

I see two brothers hugging a dog on a front lawn.

I want to remember.

But I can't.

It is too long ago.

A shepherd/collie mix, Rusty was as stately, handsome, and heroic as any dog I have ever known. His rich coat was indeed golden orange, except for the fantastic white blaze that ran down his broad and sturdy chest and the splash of white at the tip of his magnificent tail. He was my protector, my friend, my confidant, my hero. He was fiercely loyal and used to do battle with any dog that crossed the line of our property. He was serious and very task-oriented but never turned down an offer for a good wrestle on our front lawn.

He never got sick. Occasionally he would come home a bit banged up after a fight with his neighborhood rival, a street-tough little mutt named Frankie. But he always recovered quickly, and after a few days' rest he would be back outside making sure our yard was a safe place for my brother and me to have a catch.

Mom swears he never had a flea in his life.

He didn't appreciate being asked to do dog tricks. Every now and then he would begrudgingly shake your hand if you pestered him long enough.

Kisses?

Never.

My dad did dress him up once as the disguised wolf from Little Red Riding Hood. He valiantly obliged for one snapshot. I never told him it made the local paper.

He loved to chase cars. After one particular close

call, I screamed and yelled and begged him to stop. I told him I didn't want to see him die. I was eight years old. He never did it again.

He would regularly disappear, sometimes for as long as three days. Mom would worry and fret. Dad would say he was just visiting his girlfriend. Then out of the blue he would show up at the bus stop, greet us with a smile and a wag or two, then escort us home. We never did find out where he went.

Once, he broke up a fight between me and the neighborhood bully. He was the big brother I never had, the childhood angel who watched over me at all times. He was truly a gift from God.

So on those nights when Dad would come up and close the closet door, I would always ask him to do one more thing—to call Rusty upstairs to stay with me. He would yell, "Rusty! Come here boy!" Soon, I would hear his generous paws loping up the stairs. He would greet us with a smile and a wag or two and then dutifully jump up on the end of my bed, heave a hefty sigh, and fall asleep. And if the ceilings started playing tricks on me, or if doorknobs started to turn or curtains became ghostly, all I had to do was reach out with my toes and feel the warmth of Rusty's back, and I would know an angel was nearby.

A few weeks after Rusty died, my brother dreamed that Rusty flew in his bedroom window and sat on the end of his bed. My brother sat up and, to his amazement, Rusty started talking to him. They talked for a long time, about all the good times he had with our family. Then he said it was time for him to go. He flew out the window into the night.

Just like angels do.

MARGARITA

....

ON MY FIRST DAY AS A TEACHER AT THE HELEN Woodward Animal Center, I was given a warning.

"Try to stay away from the lobby on Tuesdays and Thursdays."

Since I have always been the boy who had to find out for himself that the stove was hot by touching the burner, I went to the lobby on Tuesday that first week. I can appreciate now that the staff was only trying to protect me.

Tuesdays and Thursdays are "surrender" days at the center, when dogs are returned or given up for adoption. They are the days of bowed heads, forms to fill out, and tearful explanations. They are the days of being left behind.

The days of walking away.

Those first few days burrowed deep into my soul and tested the boundaries of patience, compassion, and forgiveness.

Dog owners came with many reasons: I don't have enough time. He has too much energy. We're moving out of state.

For the first few weeks, I condemned every man and woman who walked through those lobby doors.

And then I remembered how close I had come to walking through those doors myself.

When I first adopted my golden retriever, Canyon, and he turned out not to be the perfect dog, I debated for weeks about walking away.

Tuesdays and Thursdays between 10:00 and 2:00 settled that debate. Once you see the fear, bewilderment, and confusion in the eyes of those left behind, you're changed forever.

I made it a point to sit with the newcomers. Some of them came with memories of home: a blanket, a chew toy, a bone.

Some trembled in corners. Others sat motionless, deaf to my tender words and blind to my outreached hands. A few would bounce off the bars and walls, spinning and panting as if they were trying to jump out of their own skins and misfortune. Still others were filled with fury. They were the barers of teeth, the angry barkers and growlers. I used to think of them as the bad dogs, but as time went on I began to see them as the brave warriors. I cheered their defiance and hailed their outrage.

Many dogs don't eat for the first few days. Margarita hadn't eaten for five. A young shepherd/collie/retriever mix, her deep-brown coat was shaggy and full, a wire brush wonderland of tangles and curls. I got the feeling that she was the kind of dog that would still look scruffy no matter how many times you bathed her. Perhaps it was the rogue splashes of black fur throughout her coat or the dark markings around her mouth and nose that made her look so perpetually disheveled. Her appearance was both sad and endearing.

The first time I met Margarita I could tell she was extremely bright and intelligent. Her head was cocked to the side, and she had a look in her eyes that said, "Will someone just explain to me what's going on?" So I sat with her. She sniffed me for a good, long time. A thorough background check. I like that investigative quality in a dog. When she was finished, she probably knew what I had eaten for breakfast that morning.

I find the first moments of meeting a new dog so gloriously suspenseful and fascinating. I treasure the baby steps. It is a wonder to watch the tender birth of a relationship. How often I rush headlong into things at the expense of those first moments or walk away too soon.

I leaned back against the concrete wall. I folded my

arms and crossed my legs to let her know I wasn't going anywhere soon. I pointed to her food dish. I told her about the column of ants that was rapidly approaching from the northwest. She sat down. She looked at me. She looked at the dish. She looked back at me. She slowly walked over to her bowl and began to eat. She would glance at me between bites and if I shifted my body in any way, she would stop. She would look at the gate and then back at me. She licked her bowl clean, took a couple sips of water, lay down next to me, and let out a five-day sigh.

One autumn night, I was resting in our living room. It was around 9:30 and my daughter, who was eight at the time, was in her bedroom. She was reading a scary story. She suddenly called out, "Daddy?!? . . ."

"Yes honey?"

"Ohhh . . . nothing," she replied.

She was just checking to see if I would be there for the scary parts.

I sat with Margarita for a while that afternoon. Just to let her know someone would be there that day, for the scary parts.

SABLE SUE

....

I HAVE THIS RECURRING DREAM IN WHICH I'M standing in my high school locker room after having just finished gym class. It's the last day of school. Everyone is cleaning out their lockers, showering, getting dressed, laughing, joking, and leaving. Except me.

I'm standing in front of a bank of gray lockers. I can't remember which one is mine, but I know it's in this general area. I think there are some things inside my locker that I don't want to leave behind, but I'm not sure. Fortunately, only a couple lockers have locks on them, so finding mine shouldn't be too difficult. There's only one problem—I don't know the right combination. By this time, everyone is gone. I sit down on a damp wooden bench and hang my head in despair.

If only I knew the right combination.

I would like to believe that there is a perfect home for every dog in the world. That the right combination is always just a moment away. During my time at the animal center, I always tried to keep my hopes high even for the most desperate dogs. Despite my enthusiasm, there were always a few for whom I didn't think we would ever find the right combination. But time and time again, I watched as tiny miracles took place every day.

For Nike, a frantic young German shepherd pup who was terrified of children, we found the right combination in a childless young couple who understood the time and patience he needed.

I had all but given up on Puppy Girl, a wild-eyed black shepherd/retriever mix who spent most of her time in her kennel spinning, barking, and charging the bars. But one afternoon, we found the right combination for her in a quiet, middle-aged man who said she reminded him of his childhood dog.

And for Newton—a 130-pound lovable, slobbering goliath of a bloodhound who spent most of his time knocking people over—we found the right combination in a big ex-football player who was strong enough to handle him yet gentle enough to give him the attention and care he needed.

Others, I worried about. Pooh-Bear and Bandita. Tara and Cody. Brandon and Frazier.

And Sable Sue.

Sable Sue had been at the center for almost three years, longer than any other dog. As fragile and frightened as any dog I have ever known, Sable Sue was a boxer mix with a gentle face and forever-troubled eyes. There was an almost constant tremble in her thin body, and even the slightest noise would frighten her into a corner. She panted incessantly, always trying to catch her breath in a world full of too many surprises, too many unknowns.

I sat with her often. It's hard to sit with a dog that has known only bars and cement walls most of its life. The walls are high, like huge concrete blinders to the world outside. In the solitude of her kennel, Sable spent many hours looking for things she would never see.

I wondered if there would be a tiny miracle in her life.

My official title at the center was "humane educator." My job was to teach visiting children about pet care, responsibility, and the humane treatment of animals. In addition to giving tours of the center and giving presentations at schools, I also taught children in the summer program. During ten weeks I taught ten different groups of kids. I was constantly trying to find the most effective ways to reach them. I wanted them to be my ambassadors, my hope for the future and the many Sable Sues of the world.

I realized early on that the dogs—not I—would teach them the most important lessons.

Every Monday, I had the students "adopt" dogs for the week. Each day thereafter they would sit outside their dogs' kennels, talk to them, comfort them, and get to know them.

A boy in one of my classes had decided to adopt Sable Sue as his dog for the week. Tim was bright, witty, and difficult at times. He had been anointed by his male classmates as their prepubescent king. The Clown King—king of laughs, king of the tightrope he would walk many times with me.

As any eleven-year-old boy feeling his oats might do, he graciously accepted his coronation. On the first day of class, he immediately began testing the boundaries of his kingdom, usually with me. He walked the fine line of disrespect and crossed it many times.

When I first meet a dog in the kennels, I do not judge it on its initial bark or cower. I often stand sturdy and silent, just to let it know that, at the very least, I'm curious about its behavior. I did the same with Tim. He wisecracked me a couple times, to the nervous delight of his followers. I looked at him firmly, just to let him know that I was aware of the shots he had fired at me, but I said nothing. Some children like to test boundaries more than others. Usually there's a reason.

I noticed something change in Tim when he sat with Sable Sue. His face softened. A tenderness awakened. He spoke in respectful tones. We would sit together and talk about her pretty coat, her sad eyes. I explained to him that some dogs were stronger than others, some were weaker, and often there was a leader, a dog that everyone looked up to. I told Tim he was one of the stronger ones.

Sable had become our bridge.

In the classroom, Tim was still testing me. One afternoon, I was preparing to give an exam. At Tim's age, potential sexual innuendo is at a premium, so when I mentioned that anyone caught looking at another student's test papers would be "penalized," I saw Tim's roundtable knights look to him in eager anticipation. He looked at me and then quietly wrote his name on the top of the exam. I turned and walked triumphantly back toward my desk. A low mutter came from behind. A smattering of chuckles. I turned and looked at Tim. He had a little smile on his face.

Progress, not perfection.

On Fridays, the children wrote letters to the dogs they had adopted for the week and then read them to the class. Their letters were remarkable testimonies to the inherent sensitivity that children have toward animals. To hear words like "I love you with all my heart" over and over again makes me believe that the future is in good hands. It also tells me that dogs are invaluable partners in helping us to discover or rediscover a place where we can love "with all our hearts."

Tim was the last student to read his letter. His entourage was restless and wired, anxious to roll and tumble out of their seats in laughter at Tim's first utterance. He walked up to the front of the class and began.

> Dear Sable,
>   I know what it is like to live in an orphanage. I used to be an orphan. If I can get adopted, I know you can too.
>
> > With all my heart,
> > Tim

Tiny miracles.

HONEY

....

G RAM SMOKED TWO AND A HALF PACKS OF VICEROYS a day, drank Dewar's scotch old-fashioneds, and could spout off a litany of off-color jokes at holiday time that would make Lenny Bruce flinch. She did everything she wasn't supposed to do and lived to be eighty-two. She had a great smoker's laugh, and she laughed often. She was cheery and good-natured and didn't complain much. Being a former high-fashion model in the Roaring Twenties, she was vain, self-centered, and not particularly giving or charitable. She had a rather comical habit of giving family members used birthday and holiday cards with the old names crossed out and hers written in. Funny thing was, we never said anything about them.

It was common for my mom to receive Gram's used pocketbooks or wallets as "new" Christmas gifts, wrapped in paper from the previous year, of course. I like to think that Gram was a visionary—the Grandmother of Recycling.

As a boy, I used to love to watch her smoke. It was like watching an artist at work. At the beginning of the evening, she would set her wares upon the old cobbler's bench in front of the couch. She kept her cigarettes in an elegant leather case with gold snaps at the top. Her silver lighter was heavy and worn with use, her round ashtray crystal and thick. I marveled at her ability to carry on a conversation as her long fingers opened the case and gently tapped out the small rolls of tobacco. Like a concert pianist, she would begin these smoking sonatas never once needing to look down at the keys. She would slowly bring the cigarette to her mouth, never breaking stride in a sentence or thought, raise that magnificent lighter, flip the cap with a clink, and light the flame with a sturdy snap of her thumb. The paper and tobacco would crackle as she drew in her first puff, and the sweet aroma of butane lingered in the air as she closed the cap of her lighter and gently set it down on the bench. The first movement of her recital was finished.

She drank too much. She would often send my father back to the kitchen to make her a "real drink."

"Put some booze in it this time," she'd chide.

She would finish the Sunday *Times* crossword in twenty minutes. Usually in pen.

"What the hell do I need an eraser for?" she'd say.

I never saw her cook. She was a blue-collar prima donna. I don't remember her being ill natured or mean. She just expected the world to revolve around her. If it didn't, no big deal. She'd just sit back and light up another Viceroy.

A few months after my childhood dog, Rusty, died, my mom and dad got a golden retriever. They named her Honey, a name associated with sweetness, humility, and love. I understand that any dog brought into my family after Rusty died would predictably have had a tough row to hoe, particularly with me. But like Gram, Honey expected the world to revolve around her twenty-four hours a day. She was haughty and demanding, and if you refused to give her attention, she would stand stubbornly at your feet and wait until you pet her. She was golden gorgeous and she knew it.

My dad didn't help matters much. He doted upon her every wish. He used too many P-words around her: Precious. Pretty Princess. Priceless.

"How about 'Pathetic'?" I would chime in, regarding their behavior.

They both, of course, ignored me.

In many families, well-defined allegiances develop between family members and pets. In our home, the relationships are clear: Canyon is my dog. Cielo is my wife's dog. Brodie is my daughter's dog. And though these alliances may blur at times—especially if one of the dogs decides to dig up a rosebush or ransack the trash barrels ("Look what *your* dog did!")—there's no doubt that the next time a thunderstorm rolls around, Canyon will be sitting on my head, Cielo will be nesting under the covers by Linda's feet, and Brodie will be curled up on the end of Hayden's bed.

Honey was my father's dog. There was no doubt about it. I had really tried with her. But when she came into my life, Rusty had recently died, and I was in my freshman year of college, living away from home for the first time. I would never have day-to-day interaction with her—the filling of her dog bowl, the walks around the block, the calling of her name—all the simple activities that make for a deeper connection and bond. I never really got to know her.

The truth is, the memory and legacy of Rusty was too strong. I realized that it would be many years before I could let another dog into my heart.

Gram died one rainy spring morning in 1983. I was living in New York and my modeling career was at its peak. My face could be found on the covers of magazines, on posters in the subway, and on the sides of city buses. I was young and too busy making money to recognize other priorities.

On the day of her funeral it was raining very hard, and I used that as an excuse not to attend.

"Can you imagine what the Long Island Expressway is going to be like in this rain?" I asked my mother. "Besides, I have an important audition today."

Before I moved to California, I paid a visit to her grave. My wife and I picked an unusually mild March day, the kind of early spring day where you can almost feel the eager stirrings of crocuses and hyacinths beneath your feet. We stopped at the cemetery office, got a map, and went in search of her site. We walked for a long while. We did not bring flowers.

We finally found her grave.

I have visited the graves of all my grandparents. My mom's mother and father are buried in Florida. My dad's father is buried in Brooklyn. It is an important thing to do.

I knelt and spoke about a selfish young man who had been too busy to go to her funeral. I told her how much I missed her jokes and recycled gifts. Just as I was about to leave, I saw a bunch of old plastic flowers in the middle of the path that had obviously blown off someone else's site.

There was only one thing to do.

CHAMP

....

FRIEND RECENTLY TOLD ME THAT HE HAD ADOPTED
A dog from a shelter.

"What kind?" I asked.

"Oh, I don't know," he replied. "One of those brown ones."

For every purebred Labrador and springer spaniel with papers that comes through the center, there are hundreds of "brown ones." They are the forgotten dogs. If we only knew of the treasures hidden behind their common coats and unremarkable features, perhaps we would not pass by so quickly. Whereas the frisky dalmation or the adorable teacup poodle may get adopted in a matter of hours or days, the brown ones may have to wait weeks or months for someone to even stop in front of their kennels.

I used to pass them by, too. Until I met Champ.

I would like to say that my love for dogs is unflinchingly democratic, that I have no favorites and that I love them all equally. To some degree, this is true. To misquote Will Rogers, I have never met a dog I didn't love. But I have had a special connection with some more than others. Often, it is born out of a feeling or moment I cannot explain, control, or measure.

I call it the magic connection.

A very personal and powerful exchange takes place in the search for a dog. It is why getting a dog for someone else is usually not a good idea. As people walked through the kennels, I found it very hard not to force my own favorites or preferences on them. When I stepped back and watched the process unfold, I learned a valuable lesson.

Sometimes we choose our dogs.

Sometimes they choose us.

Champ was one of the brown ones and right from the beginning we had a magic connection. He had spent most of his two-year life at the shelter, been adopted out twice and returned each time.

"Required too much attention," was the explanation of both owners.

Only when I took the time to stop in front of his kennel did I discover how beautiful Champ really was. A

shepherd/Doberman mix, he was like a gazelle in stature, long-legged and lithe. He moved with the strength and grace of a greyhound with a gorgeous lope, his body athletic and handsome. His coat was the typical blandish blend of blacks and browns, and his ears hung goofily from his good, strong head. His almond eyes were eager and alive. Through all his hopes and disappointments, he never turned bitter or angry. He seemed to carry in him an inextinguishable flame of hope. He adored children and they loved him. He dived and leaped into everything including people, perpetually distracted and thrilled by life and all it has to offer. He was like the boy who stands at the very edge of the Grand Canyon while his parents scream in horror behind the railing.

Forever playful and curious, Champ was usually found standing on the thin ledge of his kennel where the upper glass enclosure meets the lower concrete wall. There, he would balance for hours, peering over the glass to catch a glimpse of the outside world. Such fragments of life nourished his flame of hope.

On a recent visit to a California mission, I was struck by the beauty and quiet of the courtyards and gardens. But the high walls disturbed me. Although the world is harsh at times—unforgiving, unfair—interaction with life often brings opportunities to find true peace and happiness. The security behind walls is very alluring, but it pales in light of the adventures beyond.

Some dogs seem to accept walls better than others. Champ was not one of them.

One Saturday morning, I had this really strong need to see Champ. So my daughter and I jumped into our van and quickly drove to the center. When we arrived, we were told that Champ was at the hospital. A few hours earlier, he had broken the glass above his ledge and it had taken a deep slice out of his leg. His paw was bandaged and his eyes told me it hurt. I called him a big dope.

Someone told me that he had been trying to escape, but I knew he was only trying to get a better view.

On mornings when I take my dog, Canyon, for a walk around the neighborhood, I pass a garden that is dry and neglected and doesn't seem to get enough attention. But somehow it survives. In the middle of this garden is a small cactus—young, but it stands in confidence. Confident that no matter how little care or water it receives, it will continue to grow. It is not a boisterous showing. I have never seen it flower. But it never gives up reaching for the sky. I admire it every time I pass.

It is my favorite garden on the street.

CHAZ AND
SUNSHINE

....

A FEW WEEKS AFTER MY WIFE AND I CELEBRATED OUR
fifteenth wedding anniversary, she came into the
kitchen one morning while I was feeding the dogs. Just as
she was about to leave for work, she turned to me and
said, "It's all about sticking together, isn't it?"

I paused for a moment. As usual, I tried to come up
with something better. But I couldn't. I smiled.

"I think you're right," I said.

I first met Linda in Milan, Italy, in a small café in the
spring of 1980. I was the all-American boy from New
York on his first trip out of the country, on a modeling
assignment for *L'uomo Vogue*. She was the seasoned world
traveler from California who had spent the last two years

living and modeling in Paris and Munich. I was twenty-six. She was twenty-three. I wore khakis, penny loafers, and crewnecks. She was partial to Mickey Mouse mini-skirts, red pumps, and Betty Boop pocketbooks. I planned to rescue this outrageous but troubled little West Coast gypsy and whisk her back to Long Island to a world of backyard barbecues and perfect families. She liked the idea.

One year later we were married.

It never should have worked. And for long stretches it barely did. But we stuck together.

Just like Chaz and Sunshine.

It's not uncommon to have pairs of dogs surrendered to the center. Shadow and Spirit came as brother and sister. Roofey and Jonesy came as boyfriend and girl-friend. In the case of Chaz and Sunshine, there was no doubt about their relationship. They came as husband and wife. Imagine Jessica Tandy and Hume Cronyn—with fur.

They had been adopted from the center six years earlier and returned because their owners were moving out of state. Of all the dogs that were returned to the center their return was the hardest for me to accept. Yet, despite being left behind at such an old age, they demon-strated a remarkable feeling of acceptance and dignity. They were an inspiration to us all.

Chaz was a big, barrel-chested Akita mix. Gentle, quiet, and occasionally grumpy, he had one purpose in

life: to watch over Sunshine. They had been together for almost seven years, which translates to almost fifty human years of companionship. He was still crazy about her, and it showed. Every time I entered their kennel, I had to pass his inspection. There was no visiting Sunshine without his permission. He would give my legs and hands and crotch a thorough sniffing—if everything checked out, he would slowly escort me to her blanket. He would stand there and wait patiently until my visit was over.

I had never been chaperoned by a dog before.

Chaz attended to Sunshine's every need. If other dogs got too rough with her in the playfield, he would let them know it with a quick snap or cranky growl. He would also occasionally bark at children passing by their kennel, especially if they were making too much noise.

"Keep it down ya little whippersnappers!!" he'd say. "Can't ya see the little lady is trying to take a nap?"

He was just taking care of his woman.

The object of his abiding love and affection was a nine-year-old retriever/bloodhound mix. Reserved and faithful, Sunshine often feigned frailty in light of all Chaz's pampering, but she knew very well how to take care of herself. If I happened to give Chaz a little more attention than I gave her, she would quietly walk over, shoo him away, rest her chin on my lap, and politely demand her fair share of head scratches.

Despite Chaz's attention to her, a perpetual sigh flickered from Sunshine's droopy eyes that spoke either of her breed or of the reflections of a life filled with disappointment and heartache. One might imagine her as a middle-aged woman sitting in a rocking chair with a book of Emily Dickinson poems in her lap, staring out a rain-soaked window, sipping tea, waiting for her underpaid and overworked husband to return from work.

It was a joy to watch their dance and to see how much they relied upon each other every day to make it through. Their dependence was not a weakness. They just knew that they didn't have the strength to do it alone.

Perhaps the greatest turning point of my fifteen-year marriage was when we both realized that we didn't have the strength to do it alone. We stopped pretending that, at any time, if we really wanted, we could walk away.

We finally admitted that we needed each other.

We closed the escape hatch of our marriage and began to celebrate what we were instead of berating each other for what we were not. We stopped waiting for things to change in each other that would never change. We stopped expecting things from each other that we weren't capable of doing.

We started accepting each other for who we were. It took me fifteen years, but I finally realized that no matter how many times I lectured Linda, she would lock her keys in her car at least twice a year and have to call me from some distant shopping center. Usually during the final seconds of a Knicks game. And it took her fifteen years to realize that no matter how many times she reminded me, I would leave twenty-nine lights on in the house at all times.

We are partners for life, and we depend on each other every day to make it through.

In other words, we stick together.

Just like Chaz and Sunshine.

SQUEEZE

....

A T THE EASTERNMOST TIP OF LONG ISLAND IS A sleepy little fishing village, the kind of town that can easily cast a spell over anyone who passes through it. Twenty years ago, it captured my heart. And even though I live almost three thousand miles away from her quiet streets and tender beaches, all I have to do is close my eyes and I am there. Montauk will always be my sanctuary. Memories of her will forever give me comfort, solace, and peace.

Montauk was also where many of my most meaningful adventures would begin.

At a New Year's Eve party there, a modeling agent

convinced me to come to New York to shoot some pictures. Six months later I was on the cover of *Gentleman's Quarterly*. Montauk is where my wife and I celebrated our marriage and spent our honeymoon. Montauk is where I learned to surf, a passion that I carry with me still.

It would also be where we would adopt our first child—of the four-legged variety.

Her name was Squeeze. She had been scheduled to spend the rest of her life on a tuna boat. Until my wife and I showed up at the docks with a three-by-five index card from the local supermarket that said FREE HUSKY/LAB PUPPIES. We were in Montauk for the weekend, taking a break from the midsummer heat of our apartment in New York, and getting a puppy was the last thing on our minds that day. We had planned on just picking up some charcoal and lighter fluid.

She would be the first dog I would let into my heart since Rusty died.

Her mother had been hit by a car and killed only a few days earlier. She would be afraid much of her life.

She was lively and playful with her littermates, and we fell in love with her tiny brown eyebrows and frisky bark. Her owner said that a fisherman was supposed to pick her up the following week. I guess she didn't believe him. She let us take her.

Being that Squeeze was our first child, we did all the things that young parents do. We spoiled her. We constantly spoke to her in high-pitched tones and baby talk,

and brought her into our bed at the first hint of a cry or whine. Our lives revolved around her.

Raising a puppy is remarkably similar to raising a baby, especially for the first few months. Priorities change quickly. Things like housebreaking become the center of one's day. Particularly when you live in a ninth-floor apartment in Manhattan, three blocks from the nearest patch of grass, and your dog has a urinary tract infection and can't control her bladder. We chose to carpet our entire apartment with the Sunday *New York Times* for a month to deal with that little problem. It gave a whole new meaning to the term "paper training" your dog.

We bought her a bed. She never slept in it.

We bought her lots of chew toys. She wanted my slippers.

We bought her expensive dog food. She preferred the trash (she especially liked licking the bottoms of empty tuna cans).

She was stubborn, independent, and strong willed. Just like her new owners.

She once ripped apart an entire sofa just because we didn't take her along shopping for groceries. One evening we had the audacity to go for a walk around the neighborhood without her. While we were gone, she decided that our ficus tree needed repotting and she was going to help.

The vet said she was suffering from separation anxiety. I think she was just pissed off.

She was fearful and insecure. She was hardheaded. She didn't like to be left behind. She was high maintenance. She required a lot of love and attention.

She reminded me a lot of myself.

There were many days, especially in the beginning, when I felt completely overwhelmed.

Before she came into my life, I had never taken care of anyone except myself. I was unprepared for the intrusions, the inconveniences, the demands. I wanted the walks in the woods, the hours of fetch, the faithful companion. Without having to do the work. Without having to change myself.

I had just as many lessons to learn as she did.

I had very high expectations of Squeeze. I wanted her to be many things she was not. I would often apologize for her fearful behavior in the presence of company or guests. I wanted her to be brave. I wanted her to be confident. I wanted her to be relaxed and sure.

I wanted her to be the perfect dog.

I have since realized that it was the imperfections and the things she wasn't that made our time together so rich and meaningful.

I don't think Squeeze liked living in New York very much. It was just too intense for her fragile psyche. I'm sure she longed to be retrieving ducks in the snow instead of dodging buses on Broadway.

We eventually moved to the suburbs. She seemed much happier amid the tree-lined streets and gray squirrels. We both loved to go for after-dinner strolls around the neighborhood and play catch in the yard, but what we would come to treasure most was our walks in the woods.

Oh, how we walked! Hours and hours. Trail upon trail. We must have covered every trail in northern New Jersey in the first few months alone. Squeeze never ran too far ahead or lagged too far behind. Sometimes she would get brave and disappear around a bend or over the crest of a hill, but she would always come back, just close enough to make eye contact with me.

It was our little dance of love.

Unlike her soon-to-be-housemate, Brodie, Squeeze rarely chased the wild things. In fact, quite the contrary. One afternoon while we were out walking, our crackling footsteps flushed a grouse out of the underbrush a few feet in front of us. I have never seen a dog run so fast—in the opposite direction.

Thunderstorms terrified her. She usually ended up in the bathtub or sitting in my lap at the first hint of a rumble.

Yet despite her fears, she was always courageous enough to give up the security of a familiar corner or bed to tackle another adventure or move to another town. I will be forever grateful to her for all the sacrifices she made for our young, restless family.

She withstood the most difficult times in our marriage, when screaming arguments and slamming doors were almost an everyday occurrence. She graciously and patiently accepted our baby daughter into the family after almost five years of being our single pride and joy. She welcomed new dogs and cats into our home without a complaint.

She was also one of the great snorers. She would fall asleep in the middle of the living room floor, and within five minutes everyone would know. She seemed to dream a lot. Her legs would jerk, her face would twitch, and she would whine and squeak and snort like an old steam loco-motive. I used to joke that she was dreaming about having to move to Tornado Alley or about becoming a storm chaser.

She loved the snow. Many times, I would look out the window during a snowstorm and find her rolling on her back with joy or bounding through snowdrifts. In those moments she seemed the most happy and free.

She had the remarkable ability that many dogs pos-sess of retrieving a ball and keeping it one centimeter out of my reach at all times. She would toy with me for hours. Sometimes, I would pretend to quit the game, then sur-prise her by whirling around and trying to grab the ball from her mouth. She rarely fell for my little schemes.

When we moved to our farm in the country, while Brodie chased deer in the meadow Squeeze would wander off, usually in search of trash barrels set out for garbage trucks. Despite her cultured beginnings on the Upper

West Side of Manhattan, she would always be trash dog at heart.

I worried often, thinking each time that this would be the day she would never return. But she would always skulk back up the driveway at dusk, haunches quivering quite theatrically, and she'd be wincing with guilt. I'd go through my usual monologue even though we both knew that there was no stopping some private missions.

We journeyed together for ten years. Through miscarriages and midlife. In elevators and across city streets. Through snow-laden fields and beneath fiery autumn canopies of sugar maple and oak. It can be so blessedly simple and divine. A man and his dog. The things many people dream of.

In the summer of 1992, we asked her to make one more move. And it was a difficult one—New York to California. Seven days together in a Ryder rental truck. Two dogs, two cats, one five-year-old child, and two adults in search of a new life. It has taken me a long time to forgive myself for maybe asking one move too many.

One Sunday morning in early October, I walked to the kitchen. I put one and a half scoops of dry food in her dish. The newly shampooed carpets beneath my feet were finally dry. I felt bad that she had to sleep in the garage that night.

I dampened her food with warm water and then opened the door to the garage.

Sometimes, I can still see her lying there. Too still. Too quiet. I have to focus on something else. Reach for Linda's hand. Look for a sliver of moonlight.

Friends are very kind. They assure me that she died peacefully in her sleep . . .

She wasn't supposed to die so soon. We expected her to live to be very old. Our daughter would be a teenager. We would be living in the country again, where it was quiet and peaceful and there would be many trails.

And when it was time for her to go, I would be there.

Dear God, I would be there.

BRODIE

....

IN THE FALL OF 1985, MY WIFE AND I BOUGHT OUR first home on a quiet suburban street in a lovely town in northern New Jersey. A thirty-year-old Dutch Colonial, it needed a lot of work—but we were young, healthy, and full of dreams. We pruned lilacs and wallpapered bedrooms. We stripped oak floors and chopped wood. Instead of trips to the movies we made trips to the hardware store.

My modeling career had evolved into an acting and TV commercial career that was really beginning to take off. The commute to New York City was not as bad as I had imagined it would be, and my wife was almost three months pregnant. We spent our weekends in search of old dressers that needed refinishing and the perfect place to have breakfast.

Squeeze had discovered the joys of porpoising through piles of autumn leaves, and our new woodstove promised to keep our home warm and cozy for the winter. The orange glow that had always welcomed me home on dusky Sunday afternoons when I was a boy was now calling me from new windows.

Life was as close to perfect as it had ever been.

When I got off the train one blustery Wednesday afternoon and saw Linda's face through the windshield of our car, I knew something was wrong. She was crying from a place I had never known her to cry from before. When I got into the car, she sobbed, "Oh my God. . . . I'm losing my baby."

As we drove to the hospital, I got pulled over for speeding. I frantically explained to the officer what was going on. He offered to give us a police escort. So with lights flashing and sirens wailing, we raced through red lights and busy intersections.

Those were my first real moments as an adult. Up until then, I hadn't realized that even at the age of thirty, I was still depending on the strength and wisdom of my parents to carry me through life. I had never made the break. Now I was being asked to draw on strength and courage I wasn't quite sure I even had.

In that speeding car I made the break. And the strength and courage came.

At the hospital, I learned that it was fairly common for first pregnancies to end in miscarriage. A few weeks later, while working in the basement, I fell to my knees and cried from a place that I had never cried from before.

Four months later, Linda was pregnant again. The first three months were very tense. Any unusual twinge or cramp filled us with worry. So we tried to fill that huge gap of uncertainty and fear with projects and activities.

And another dog.

We had talked about getting a companion for Squeeze. But she had become so used to being the center of attention that we worried about how she would react to a new baby in the house.

"It's time to turn her back into a dog again," I said.

So we searched for a friend for Squeeze and another spirit to help us through the last six months of Linda's pregnancy.

At a cold and crowded shelter in Linden, New Jersey, we found Brodie.

She was curled up like a pincushion in the corner of her kennel. A collie/shepherd mix, she was thin and hungry. I knelt down and called to her. She shyly approached me with world-weary eyes that spoke of a deep sadness. I immediately felt a connection. One hour later she was sitting between me and Linda on the front seat of our Dodge pickup. Judging from her behavior once we got home, I am tempted to say that her performance at the shelter had been nothing short of Oscar quality. We were to learn that behind that veil of timidity and fear was a stubborn, hell-raising, passionate gal of a dog.

Little did I know of the adventures Brodie would take me on.

On September 12, 1986, at 5:30 in the afternoon, we were blessed with a healthy seven-and-a-half-pound girl. We named her Hayden Elizabeth. It was a long and difficult labor.

But the strength and courage came.

With the addition of a new child and another dog, we quickly outgrew our small home. Squeeze and Brodie had become wonderful friends and mischief-makers and needed room to run. So when Hayden was about six months old, we sold our house and moved to a seven-acre farm in the Hudson Valley about an hour outside New York City. It was a beautiful piece of land, with views to High Point State Park in New Jersey to the west and apple orchards to the south. We had always dreamed of living on a farm in the country.

Here we discovered how much Brodie loved the great outdoors. Nothing thrilled her more than to chase the white-tailed deer that foraged in the meadow below. Although she was fast, she was no match for these hypervigilant leapers and bounders. We would watch her noble but futile chases from our deck, chuckling as the deer would zigzag through the sumac and underbrush and disappear into the woods, leaving Brodie behind chasing ghosts.

She would run for hours, seemingly possessed by their phantom scent and trails. When she finally returned home, exhausted, her eyes would be wild and her tongue would be dangling around her feet. Each time, we'd figure that she had finally learned her lesson and would retire from such frivolous pursuits.

No such luck.

Like me, she would have to learn things the hard way. Perhaps that was what I had first detected in her eyes at the shelter—a deep understanding and an acceptance that her road might always be a difficult one, her life lessons sharp and unforgiving.

And often quite comical.

I was by her side for most of them. Her lessons were mine as well.

On the second night in our new home, Brodie decided to bring us a housewarming gift from the meadow. As I was taking out the trash, I heard her unmistakable yap and the crackling of twigs and branches in the underbrush. I yelled and called her, knowing damn well she wouldn't come. But after a few persistent firm growls from me, she emerged from the brush with something grayish white in her mouth. I ran toward her, arms flailing (it could have been a disposable diaper for all I knew). She dropped the object and slinked away. I shined my super-strength, city-guy-moves-to-the-country overkill flashlight on the object and was treated to an astoundingly ugly creature full of slobbery fur, fiendish eyes, and a mouth that seemed glued open baring some pretty impressive chompers.

I went through my New York City and Jersey suburban wildlife mental rolodex—rat . . . pigeon . . . squirrel . . . —and came up empty. And then, suddenly, in the deep dark sky above appeared the kind face of my seventh-grade science teacher, Mrs. Anderson. She spoke.

"Why, Gary, this is one of our little marsupial friends, the opossum. I know he may be virtually undistinguishable right now, but that is only because he has spent the last few moments in the jaws of your dog."

The wise Mrs. Anderson. She was always one of my favorite teachers.

I stood there for a while celebrating my first close encounter with a wild species. Suddenly I saw its jaws move. Not much, but just enough to confirm that he was still alive. I scolded Brodie hard for not finishing the job and decided the only humane thing to do was to put the possum out of its misery.

I grumbled as I walked back to the garage, wondering how I might complete the deed. I spotted my softball bat in the corner and decided it was the best way. The end would come swift, like a sharp single to left with the bases full in the bottom of the ninth.

I told myself it was a baptism of sorts, an initiation to the harsh realities of living among wild things. I grabbed my bat and headed outside. I set my light down on the ground so it outlined the possum's form. I took a deep breath and noticed that Brodie was watching me in a rather bemused way. Mumbling that it was all her fault, I raised the bat above my head. And just as I was ready to lower my thirty-four-ounce gauntlet, Mrs. Anderson's sweet face reappeared in the sky above. She spoke to me again.

"Now Gary, this little omnivorous and nocturnal mammal has a very clever way of protecting himself when threatened or attacked. Do you remember what they pretend to do?"

"Play dead," I answered.

I walked back to the garage, sort of chuckling, thinking about how Brodie had witnessed the whole charade with that puzzled look in her eyes. She probably got a good laugh out of the whole thing. I went outside about a half hour later to check on the possum. Sure enough, he was gone.

A few weeks later, Brodie and I were on a deep hike on state forest land. It was a paradise of scents and aromas, and she romped through the waving ferns in search of furry creatures. She ran up ahead in her usual manner, her bark indicating that she was at least lukewarm on the trail of something. All of a sudden, it became more persistent and sharp. I followed the sound into a dark grove of hemlocks and spotted her white-tipped tail wagging furiously. She had obviously cornered something. It was only after she turned around and looked at me that I learned what she had found. A porcupine had generously deposited thirty or forty quills into Brodie's snout, gums, jaw, and tongue. I screamed at her to back away, and she did. I was stunned by the number of quills in her face. I had heard stories about how most porcupine quills were barbed and almost impossible to remove without pliers. I was two miles deep into state land. I had no pliers or Swiss army knives.

Dogs know when they have messed up. You can see it in their eyes.

One by one, I pulled the quills out—from her gums, her tongue, the roof of her mouth, her nose, and her chin. She never resisted. She never cried.

To be held in such trust is a great honor. It is the same trust a child bestows upon his or her parents.

How often we run from that sacred responsibility.

After I finished pulling out the last quill, we sat together under the hemlocks for a while.

She looked at me with those sad eyes.

"C'mon girl," I said. "Let's go home."

That night when we pulled into the driveway, Brodie didn't bolt into the meadow when I opened the door. She slowly stepped out of the car and dutifully waited for me by the front door. I was convinced she had finally learned her lesson.

• • •

One week later she got skunked. A few weeks after that she held a raccoon hostage for a couple hours at the top of a spindly cherry tree. Soon thereafter she got skunked again.

I wondered what it would take for her to change her ways.

That fall, we decided to limit our walks to the woods behind our farm. There, Brodie could chase chattering chipmunks and gray squirrels instead of porcupines, and I could calm my nerves.

The forest has always been my church, my sanctuary, my sacred refuge. Walking in the woods has always been a holy act for me, be it a casual stroll or grueling day hike. It is where I feel safe, protected, and truly at home.

So when a hunter shot off Brodie's front paw one snowy November morning in the woods behind our farm, I was a homeless man in a world gone mad.

It was a deliberate act. She had been shot at point-blank range in protest of our interference with the hunter's quest for white-tailed deer. I found Brodie sitting quietly under a small oak, her right paw dangling by a thread. I cradled her in my arms, took off one of my gloves, unlaced my boot, and secured the glove around her paw. I carried her for half a mile out of the woods to our home.

She was heavy. I kept tripping on rocks and

branches hidden in the snow. The gunshot rang over and over in my disbelieving ears.

The vet said that if the shotgun blast hadn't cauterized all the blood vessels at the site of the wound, she would have bled to death.

For weeks I found myself sitting at traffic lights plotting my revenge. Suddenly, everyone in town that drove a pickup truck became a suspect. Many nights I drove around the countryside searching for answers I would never find.

That spring, I went back and stood at the edge of those woods. I wasn't ready to go back in, but all the pain of that November day poured out of my soul and the sound of my screams ricocheted off every shagbark hickory and hemlock.

As time goes on, the anger diminishes and the wounds begin to heal in the light of forgiveness, acceptance, and humility and the knowledge that our species is a lot less advanced than we might care to believe.

Brodie is about twelve years old now. She has slowed down a bit but gets around fine on her three and a half legs. Every now and then, when I take her into the woods, she gets that old gleam in her eyes. But she is finished chasing things she cannot catch.

And so am I.

TIFFANY

....

IT IS DIFFICULT TO EXPRESS THE FEELINGS OF excitement and dread that come over you when you watch your child's first wobbly footsteps. It is the beginning of your understanding that for the next six months you will live your life in a perpetual state of lunging and preparing to lunge. Every item in the house suddenly becomes a potential head-splitter. Coffee table corners are now the enemy, stairs in any form trigger panic attacks, and thick-lipped area rugs on wood floors become the stuff of nightmares. Single-story ranch homes with carpeting and upholstered couches become havens for weary nerves. I can understand why my mom leaned a little to the overprotective side. Most likely, she saw a look in my eyes. A look of longing for things beyond. And for adventure. She was probably just trying to hold on for as long as she could.

Those first steps are also the beginning of a lifelong process of letting go. I have seen the same look in my daughter's eyes that my mom must have seen in mine. I have also noticed that when we go for walks together on trails in the woods, she runs up ahead a little farther each time. I want to call her back, and sometimes I do. But often I don't. Because down that trail, out of my sight, is where most of her adventures lie.

Tiffany had decided that it was time for an adventure. A shy and unassuming beagle/rottweiler mix, she was the last dog at the animal center I would have figured for making a breakout. She had never caused trouble in the past. She was quiet and extremely well behaved. She was polite on her leash, rarely barked, and always came when called.

Little did we know that she had been practicing for weeks how to open her kennel gate.

She must have known that the kennel techs were leaving the main door to her barracks partially open at night. She also must have known that the janitor finished cleaning the main building around 7:30. And that he drove a 1977 Volvo with no muffler.

I can only imagine how it all happened. Around

8:00 one Friday night, her adventure began. She jumped up on her gate, pressed her nose against the bars, and flicked up the latch with her paw. The gate swung open with a resounding crash against the concrete wall.

She raced down the hall to the barracks door. It was partially open, but not far enough for her to squeeze through. So she pushed. And squeezed. And pushed. And squeezed. Each time, the massive door opened a little more. Finally, there was enough room to push through.

She could feel the cool night air on the tip of her nose. She romped across the grounds of the animal center, jumped over a fence into the field next door, and never looked back.

She had forgotten how wonderful the wild grasses felt rushing across her face. About the sound of the wind whistling in her ears. The feeling of her paws bounding on the wild earth, the taste of freedom and a life filled with adventure.

She had forgotten what it was like to be a dog.

She ran for three days and nights, exploring the many backyards in the neighborhood, taking sips from swimming pools, and weaving her way through jungle gyms and around swing sets. She ran with the children during recess at the local elementary school.

She was on an adventure.

Tiffany had always wanted to walk down Main Street off her leash. So she headed for town. She trotted past the bank and the hardware store. She flirted with a standard poodle tied to a No Parking sign next to the post office. She stopped and sniffed a bicycle tire in front of the library. She lingered a bit outside the local market, tempted by the aromas beckoning from behind the automatic sliding glass doors. A few kind faces tried to approach her, but she kept her distance. Once someone read the blue bone-shaped tag on her collar, her adventure would be over.

She still had many things to see.

Tiffany ran through fields dotted with brown-skinned men and women who wore wide-brimmed hats and put tomatoes into wooden bushel baskets. They called to her as she ran down the rows of red and green. "Perro blanca! Perro blanca!"

Their voices sounded sweet in the misty morning air.

At night, she galloped down the long, lush fairways of the golf course. The soft spray of the water sprinklers left little droplets on her long whiskers and bathed her dusty coat clean. When she got tired, she'd find a grove of pepper trees and fall asleep beneath their weeping branches to the sounds of crickets in the tall grass.

On the third day, she stepped in a gopher hole while running across a soccer field. It was time to go back.

We found her limping in a church parking lot. And while everyone examined her paw and counted cuts and bruises, I quietly rejoiced over the sparkle in her eyes.

The kind of sparkle that comes only from going on adventures.

In the summer of 1996, my ten-year-old daughter got on a plane by herself and flew to New York to visit her grandparents. Every bone in my body wanted to call her back.

When Linda and I picked her up at the airport three weeks later, she looked different. Had she grown in those three weeks? Maybe it was the new denim jacket she was wearing. Maybe it was the way her hair was parted down the middle.

Or maybe it was something in her eyes.

CODY

....

WHEN I WAS SEVEN YEARS OLD MY FATHER TOOK ME to my first baseball game. Yankee Stadium. Jerome Avenue. Subways rumbling and screeching above my head. Upper-deck seats so high that I was afraid if I leaned too far forward I would tumble over the railing into the outfield below. I held my father's hand for the first three innings.

I had never seen grass so green or lights so bright. We ate hot pretzels and potato knishes and drank Yoo-hoos. And that night, Mickey Mantle limped out of the dugout in the bottom of the ninth and pinch-hit a home run over the auxiliary scoreboard in right-centerfield to win the game.

I became forever enchanted.

You're lucky if you have a father by your side when magical things like that happen. That evening became our communion. I carry the power of that night with me to this day.

In the years to come we wouldn't say "I love you" very much. We would just talk about the Yankees.

Five years later, I was on a field trip to the ocean with my summer camp mates. Even though I was twelve, I was still very much afraid of the water. I'd walk along the shore gathering shells and looking for beach glass while my friends rode the waves and played in the surf. I wanted so badly to be out there with them. But I was stuck.

A camp counselor, who must have seen the fear in my eyes and the longing in my heart, came up to me and offered to take me out beyond the breakers. He held my hand as we waded out together. When it got too deep, he picked me up.

A very large wave loomed on the horizon. I got scared.

"I promise," he said, "that if we go under together, we'll come out the other side."

The wave came.

We went under together.

And we came out the other side.

• • •

A father takes my hand and eases my fears at a baseball game. A camp counselor dedicates twenty minutes of his life to me. These are two of the strongest memories of my childhood. Sometimes I worry about what events will find their way into my daughter's memory. Especially when I recall some of the things I have said and done over the years.

I remember one morning when Hayden was in first grade, she was giving me a particularly hard time about what she was going to wear to school that day. She rejected every one of the choices I pulled from her closet and dresser drawers. Finally, I got so frustrated that I screamed.

"That's it!! I've had enough! You're going to school naked!"

She looked at me in horror. It was the first and only time I have ever seen her lower lip quiver. She burst into tears.

I thought it was a moment that would scar her forever.

Recently, I asked Hayden if she remembered that day. She said that she didn't but that she sure thought it was funny I would say such a dumb thing.

Her response reminded me that I don't have to be a perfect parent. I will make mistakes. I will lose my patience. I will say stupid things. The most important thing is that she knows someone will be there when she can't decide between overalls and jean shorts.

• • •

Of the many breeds I saw come to the animal center, it seems that none had a more difficult time adjusting to the bars and concrete than the Labradors. The idea of being separated from human contact was almost too much for them to bear.

I took one under my wing. His name was Cody.

I was worried about Cody from the start. I had never seen a dog so desperate to get out. Surrendered as a four-year-old untrained, unneutered, and underloved black Lab, Cody was a slobbering, leaping mess of fear and panic. I couldn't imagine how anyone passing by his kennel would consider him for adoption. Yet I knew that beneath all that craziness was a wonderful dog. So he became my project. I would take temporary custody—be his interim foster parent, his accomplice to freedom.

Every day for three months, I went to see him first thing in the morning. Usually with a roll of paper towels. He would pant and slobber so much during the night that his entire neck and chest would be soaking wet. I would dry him off, talk to him softly, and try to calm him down. I usually left his kennel full of hair, slobber, and scratch marks.

I was determined to help him come out the other side.

After I cleaned him up I would take him for a walk. He loved walking out to the playfield with me. He would trot along and look up at me and smile. He never pulled on his leash and was most content staying right by my side. When we reached the field, he would lift his nose high in the air and drink in all the scents sailing on the breeze.

He was very methodical when it came to taking care of his business. He chose his spots carefully, and when he was finished he would rake his front and back claws across the ground like a bull preparing to charge. If it was an attempt to cover up what he had just deposited, he never came close.

He was black as coal, a little chubby but strong. His dark brown eyes were always hopeful and eager, and when he wagged his tail, the entire rear quarter of his body swayed from side to side like a hula dancer.

He was also a leaner. If I stopped to have a conversation with someone on my way to the field, before I knew it he would be leaning against my leg. If I sat on a bench, he would come over, sit down, and lean against my knee. When I took him to schools with me, he would lean against my shoulder as I drove.

I love it when dogs lean on me.

Every day I brought him to sit with me in my office. He was most content lying on top of my feet under my desk. This way he knew I couldn't get away without him knowing. It was the only time I ever saw him close his eyes and rest. I tried to keep my feet very still, knowing of his many sleepless nights.

Each night, under a pepper tree in my backyard, I prayed for someone to take Cody home.

One afternoon when I was working at my desk, a man poked his head around the corner of my office door and asked me where the rest rooms were.

"Around the corner to your left," I replied.

"Thanks! . . . By the way, who is that?" he said, pointing to my feet.

"Oh, that's Cody. Isn't he beautiful?"

And on that gloriously sunny day in the spring of 1996, Cody found a home and a new pair of feet to sleep on.

That summer I bought a new surfboard. And in the fall, the Yankees won the World Series.

It was a great year.

PARSON BROWN

....

H IS HISTORY READ LIKE A CRIMINAL RAP SHEET. BREED:
Jack Russell terrier. Third failed adoption. Had
bitten new owners five times. Very dominant and aggressive, particularly around food. Attacked puppy and refused to let go. Growled at kennel techs trying to clean
floors. Extremely unpredictable. Owners have "tried everything."

Except letting him be a Jack Russell terrier.

I knew twenty minutes of Parson Brown's life. He
had been returned to the center for the last time.

He had refused to eat and hadn't relieved himself for
two days. One of my co-workers said he was waiting to
"let it all go at once."

Parson Brown had become somewhat of a leper. His reputation was such that no one wanted to go near him. Bad reputations interest me. I wanted to find out for myself how horrible he really was.

So I went to see him. I slowly opened his kennel door. I carefully hooked his leash. We went for a walk together.

We walked across the parking lot on our way to the playfield. A large garbage truck pulled in the driveway. Parson froze, lifted his right front paw, pointed his stump of a tail, and assessed the situation. No immediate threat. We moved on. His gait was strong, confident, and purposeful. He began to pull a bit on his leash. I gave it a sharp tug. He respectfully slowed down. He wanted to go right; I pulled him left. We played chess with each other. I watched his moves and he watched mine. He had his reputation; I was giving him a taste of mine.

Once we arrived at the field, there was work to be done—scents to be identified, territories to be defined. Things to be protected and enemies to be found. He approached ground squirrel holes like a policeman with a warrant. Nose in. No fear. Checking the situation. He moved from hole to hole with SWAT team precision. He was patient and thorough. When he felt satisfied with his inspection, we moved on. He pulled right; I pulled left.

White queen takes black rook.

I sat on a bench under a dying tree. Parson sat at my feet. I closed my eyes and pictured a ranch in Wyoming.

Just like the photograph I have hanging in my office: thunderheads building in the western hills, red-tail hawks carving circles in the air and screaming in celebration of the endless sky above. Cattle grazing and sunflowers swaying.

I opened my eyes. Parson was looking at me. We made eye contact for the first time. I introduced myself. He did the same. I patted his side firmly and affectionately. He wagged his tail, smiled, and turned around to resume his guard over the field.

I closed my eyes again. I am back in Wyoming. The prairie wind bathes a smile across my face. The afternoon shadows are growing long and the tall grasses are tinting peach. It has taken long, but I am finally home. It's time to chop some wood for the evening fire.

Walking beside me is a small but proud hunter. He gives chase to a jackrabbit that springs from the brush, but the rabbit is too fast.

"Maybe next time," I say. "Maybe next time."

CIELO

....

I HAVE ALWAYS BEEN A BIG-DOG KIND OF GUY. MY experience with little dogs has been very limited. My mom had a rather yappy little dachshund named Juliet when I was a boy, but my memories of her are sketchy. She had this unfortunate habit of waiting in the middle of the road until my mom got home from work. One day she just didn't get out of the way fast enough.

"No one even stopped," Mom said.

My next-door neighbor had a very old pug that waddled around the house with buggy, drippy eyes and a bark that can be described only as a heavy smoker's hack in miniature. I am still convinced she was part June bug.

I grew up with an assortment of retrievers, collies, and shepherds. Dogs you could tackle on the front lawn after a long day at school or hug with all your might without fear of hurting them. I had never imagined a small dog being part of our family.

Until a little dog with a beard came into our lives.

In the fall of 1993, I decided to answer a rather ambiguous ad in a San Diego newspaper for a teaching position in Tijuana, Mexico. It was for an after-school program that taught English as a Second Language to students from surrounding schools. Although I had a bachelor's degree and some teaching experience, I didn't have all the course requirements needed to receive a California teaching credential. Unless I was willing to go back to college, I could not teach in the public school system. So I applied at the Queen Elizabeth Institute in Tijuana.

Since our arrival in California, I had abandoned my acting and modeling career and worked in jobs ranging from selling advertising to telemarketing personalized re-frigerator magnets. I was at my wit's end, unemployed, angry, and convinced that no one ever got work from the want ads. "You gotta know somebody, you gotta have connections," I wailed.

I got the job.

I would like to say that I got hired because of my sterling résumé and sparkling interview. But I learned later from one of the other instructors that the primary reason I

had been hired was that I had curly blonde hair and blue eyes.

"It is very important to the headmaster at the institute that the American teachers *look* American," he told me.

As it turned out, they were also looking for someone to teach arts and crafts. My wife had taught art in a number of summer programs.

"Don't worry," I told her while she was blow-drying her long blond hair one night after taking a shower. "You're a shoo-in."

So for the next three years, we would cross the U.S./Mexican border twice a day, four days a week.

Going into Mexico was rarely a problem. Coming back into the United States was often quite an adventure.

A very dirty and hungry dog had wrapped her paws around my wife's leg as she stood waiting in front of a shoemaker's kiosk a couple doors down from the school.

"I've never been hugged by a dog before," Linda said. "She wouldn't let go. And isn't she cute? Look at those sweet eyes! And the beard! Look at that beard!"

She did indeed have a beard. A very long and scraggly one. It was the first thing you noticed about her. I gave Linda that "last thing we need is another dog" look as she cradled the little street terrier in the school courtyard. After all, we already had two dogs and three cats.

We were soon surrounded by students. The little bearded one charmed them all. Linda told her story about how she had found her.

"She is a gift from the sky, a gift from the sky!" cried one girl.

We named her Cielo—sky.

Our plan was to hide Cielo under Linda's heavy winter coat on the floor by her feet. In our two years crossing the border, our car had rarely been searched. Most of the time we were asked a couple questions regarding our purpose for being in Mexico and whether we had anything to declare. I remembered a sign at the border checkpoint that said it was illegal to bring any *produce* or *livestock* into the States and since a fox terrier didn't fit into any livestock category I knew, we decided that we weren't breaking any laws by trying to bring her home.

We felt confident. I would remain cool, casual, and matter-of-fact. Just like on a typical night coming home from work.

We drove from the school to the border crossing at San Ysidro, passing taco stands and young men hawking everything from newspapers to fresh roses. Cielo was curled in a little ball under Linda's parka. She was quiet and still. It was as if she knew this was her only chance and wasn't about to blow it.

We jockeyed our way into the typically chaotic line of cars. Traffic was light, and in minutes we were at the checkpoint. I recognized our border agent. He asked us the usual questions.

"Teaching, sir. Yes, teaching English at the Queen Elizabeth Institute. Yes, both my wife and myself. No sir, nothing to declare this evening."

It was a flawless performance. I was brilliantly normal. I had captured and portrayed that kind of day-after-day weariness that comes from crossing the border every day. And Cielo had fallen into nothing short of a coma. Not a squirm. Not a whimper. She knew the stakes.

My wife is the kind of person who always gives away the punch line of a joke at the very beginning of its telling. And then she always wants to start over again. So when the border guard asked Linda what was under her coat, my heart went into instant arrhythmia.

In a tone of voice that would best be described as that of the village idiot, she answered, "Oh, nothing. . . . Just my big feet."

My wife is a beautiful, graceful woman. So when the guard asked her to pick up her coat and she began acting like Elmer Fudd, I knew we were doomed. He asked her to step out of the car, walked around to the passenger side, and lifted up her coat. There he found our bearded little stowaway, fast asleep.

He said nothing about it. He asked us to get back in the car and tagged a very intimidating little piece of yellow paper to our windshield. He instructed us to proceed to Secondary Inspections, where agents have been known to completely dismantle cars and vans in minutes.

The yellow piece of paper said "Hiding dog under coat." We were scared. Not so much for ourselves, but for Cielo. Even though she had found Linda only two hours earlier, she was already a part of us. We could not leave her behind.

One of my dreams when I moved to California was to hear the howl of a coyote. After dogs, they are my favorite animal. In Native legends, it is said that Coyote created the earth and carried fire down from the mountains. He was the mischief-maker, the trickster, and he could transform himself into any shape he wished. His ultimate responsibility, set down by the great Spirit Chief, was "to set things right," however he might interpret that mandate. Many of his best-laid plans and schemes didn't turn out the way he'd expected. At those times he used his trickery and cleverness to repair the situation. I thought of Coyote as we sat in that dimly lit holding area.

We waited about an hour. Finally, another border agent approached and asked us to step out of the car. She said very little—asked me to open the trunk. She poked around a bit with her flashlight and then plucked the yellow piece of paper from the windshield. She looked at it for a moment and with a wave of her hand told us to proceed across the border.

I don't think she heard a word of my story about

how I had brought "Freckles" down to Mexico to show to my class as I talked about dog physiology. Just one look at Cielo and she would have known I was lying.

I have no idea why she let us go.

Maybe she recognized a gift from the sky.

BRANDON

....

ONE DAY WHEN I WAS DRIVING ALONG A WINDING country road, a bird flew into my windshield. It hit very hard and got caught in the driver's side windshield wiper. One stunned eye stared at me through the glass.

I have rescued hummingbirds trapped in skylights. As a boy, I would save lightning bugs that flew in my bedroom window—I would hold a record album cover on the wall until they crawled onto it, and then I would quickly run to the window to set them free. I have opened every window and door in my home and waited patiently for a wasp to find its way out rather than smash it with a rolled-up newspaper. It probably has a lot to do with my upbringing. I can't remember a time when my mom wasn't nurturing some wild creature back to health or taking in a stray.

"They know I can't turn away," she'd laugh. "That's why they come here."

One of my great challenges is to know when to intervene and when to step back. I can't save everything. Besides, many times my best intentions and help may not be the best for the situation. Often, there is a bigger picture I cannot see.

One Tuesday morning, an eight-day-old puppy was brought to the center. It was bleeding heavily—its owner told us that the mother had tried to kill the puppy by biting its neck. We quickly rushed him to the hospital, where the vet repaired the six-inch wound during a two-hour operation. It was touch and go for a couple days, but the little pit bull made it.

We hand- and bottle-fed him for six weeks. He was feisty and hungry, growing steadily, and after three weeks his wound had completely healed. All signs pointed to a complete recovery.

We named him Rex.

Then one afternoon he developed a fever. His condition deteriorated quickly during the night. The vets did everything they could to save him.

He died the next morning. An autopsy revealed a massive internal infection that his immune system couldn't fight.

My first reaction when I heard the news was not of grief but of sorrow. We may have interfered in a very merciful and intimate act on the part of the mother. I thought of the baby barn swallow I had found on the ground one morning below the eaves in front of the center. Had it fallen out by accident, or had it been forced out for reasons I couldn't see? Did the mother really know that her little pup wasn't strong enough to make it? These are the humbling dilemmas that remind me of my place in the world and that some choices can be very difficult to make.

The bird that had landed on my windshield that day turned out to be a Northern flicker, a relative of the woodpecker family. I could tell by its plumage that it was a male. I quickly pulled over and untangled his wings from the wiper. I cradled the bird in my hands. He was stunned and remained very still in my grasp. His breathing was labored, and his magnificently long tongue dangled hopelessly from his mouth. I felt honored to be holding such a wild creature. I walked to a grassy area under a tree and sat with him. I admired his brilliant and radiant red crown, his speckled breast, his saberlike beak. We sat together for five minutes or so. Suddenly, his body shook. He turned his head to the side, closed his eyes, and was gone.

I had never held death before.

I set him down under a yellow forsythia, said a little prayer, and got back into my car. I kept replaying the scene in my head. Could I have swerved to avoid him? Could I have hit the brakes sooner? Why did the bird have to fly right in front of my car? What could I have done differently?

A friend told me that sometimes, no matter what we do, we can't change a thing. "I hope *I* die in someone's arms," she said.

When I first arrived at the animal center, I was determined to befriend every dog in every kennel. I thought no dog, regardless of its ferociousness or fear, would be able to resist my amazing sensitivity and healing powers. I'm lucky I don't have a chunk of my calf missing as a result of such grandiose and self-centered thinking.

Brandon was a shepherd/retriever mix. Two years old, he was handsome and lively, his coat long and feathery. His face was golden, his eyes somewhat worrisome but friendly. He had been at the shelter for about eight months. His bark was sharp and strong. I should know— he barked at me all the time.

For six months, I played missionary to Brandon's

wild Indian. He didn't budge. I made absolutely no progress with him. Each time that I approached him, his response was the same. He would back to the middle of his
kennel, set his feet, offer me a low-growled greeting, and
fire off a series of fierce and distinguished barks. He
wanted nothing to do with me. Whenever I actually tried
to go into his kennel, he let me know of his displeasure
very quickly. He would stiffen even more and the hair on
his back would rise up in deep protest.

Each day with Brandon, I was a vacuum cleaner
salesman standing in front of a freshly slammed door.

Usually after repeated visits, a dog will soften. I
tried everything with Brandon. Although he seemed more
at ease around women, he seemed fine with most men. I
tried bribing him with treats. He didn't go near them. I
pretended I didn't care, feigned aloofness, hoping he
might feel scorned. He didn't buy it. I hung out with
people he liked. They even told him I was a great guy. He
thought otherwise. I yelled back at him during his
barkathons, going for the tough love approach.

He always held his ground.

I touched him twice. Both times he got a little too
quiet and stood a little too still.

I finally gave up my quest.

One morning, I was getting ready to take a shower.
I had cleared all the daddy longlegs from the bottom of

the tub and had checked behind the shampoo and conditioners on the shelves for any additional squatters. When I determined that all of my arachnid chums had been moved to a safe place, I turned on the water. I was well into washing my hair when, all of a sudden, a medium-size spider rappelled from one of the upper creases of the shower curtain. I screamed and yelled as it quickly descended through the steam.

"Hey!!! Hey!!!! Where are you going? You're going to die if you go any farther, you idiot! Hey!!! Stop!!!!"

The bathroom door opened. It was my daughter.

"Who are you talking to Daddy?" she asked.

"Just the spiders, honey."

"Oh . . . ," she replied, and closed the door.

I tried to move the nozzle away but the spray was too wide. The spider fell to the bottom of the tub and disappeared in a swirl down the drain.

Sometimes, no matter what you do, you can't change a thing.

PATCHES

....

I ONCE ASKED A CLASS OF FOURTH GRADERS FOR A definition of the word *faith*. I received a lively assortment of ideas and responses that ranged from "having a strong belief in God" to "going to church a lot" and "trusting something you can't see." We had a remarkably interesting and insightful discussion. Just as I was about to move on to a math lesson, the quietest and most timid girl in the class raised her hand. She stood up slowly and said, "Faith is believing what is true."

I don't know whether it is biologically possible for coyotes and dogs to interbreed. A simple phone call to the San Diego Zoological Society would probably clear up any doubt. Perhaps I'll make that call someday. Until then, I'm taking it on faith. Faith in a feeling that the blood, spirit, and soul of a coyote runs deep and wild through the veins of a dog named Patches.

The card hanging on her kennel said "Australian shepherd mix." There is a joke among the kennel techs that when in doubt about identifying a midsize or larger dog breed, just write "Aussie mix." That blend seems to cover a lot of ground. To my naive eye, the somewhat brindled and speckled coat on Patches indicated Aussie blood, and her size and chronic hip dysplasia were consistent with German shepherds. But the first time I saw her, I blurted out, "Oh my God, it's a coyote!" With her long, cautious nose, keen triangular ears, bushy tail, and mysterious eyes, it's not difficult to understand why I reacted that way.

On our first meeting, she walked to the farthest corner of her kennel, turned around, sat down, and ignored me. On our twentieth meeting, she walked to the farthest corner of her kennel, turned around, sat down, and ignored me. On our fiftieth meeting, she walked to the farthest corner of her kennel, turned around, sat down, ignored me, and yawned. She didn't come near me for two months.

When I first moved to California, I wanted to connect with the Native American culture. It began as a somewhat starry-eyed search for what I believed was the ultimate wisdom. I became friends with a young Lakota man named Joshua who invited me to a sweat lodge ceremony in the high desert about two and a half hours east of San Diego. I was excited, curious, and very nervous. I imagined a grand ceremony amid magical spires of red rock, shimmering cottonwoods, and paths that led to an earthen temple draped in handwoven Navajo blankets and buffalo hides.

Josh was very patient with me.

We drove out on a cool autumn afternoon in October. As we pulled onto the reservation, I was greeted by a couple abandoned pickups, a rusted washing machine, a few old tires, a ghastly assortment of thin and barking dogs, and lots of dust. Where was the tourmaline and turquoise entrance gate? Where were the green pastures and red spires of rock? Frankly, I expected enlightenment to be much neater. Instead, the ceremony began much more like a Sunday afternoon barbecue. Cars pulled up and foil-covered dishes exchanged hands. Barefoot kids played tag in the dusty driveway and a television blared through open windows. I wanted to leave. This was not what I had read about back at the New Age bookstore.

This was too much like real life.

Josh introduced me to everyone. Most gave me a quick hello and went about their business. I immediately assumed they didn't like me. I had expected to be welcomed as a brave white brother, one who was sensitive and compassionate about all the injustices that my people had inflicted upon their people.

Josh was very patient with me.

We arrived at 4:00. The ceremony didn't begin until 7:00. Josh politely explained to me about "Indian time."

"Take the time they say we will get started," he laughed, "and add two hours to that!"

I would have laughed, but I was too busy staring at the sweat lodge, a small domelike structure covered in dirty blankets and old carpeting. Where were the hand-woven Navajo blankets? The buffalo hides? And was that an old refrigerator down in the dried-up riverbed?

Suddenly, the mood changed. It was time. A group of about fifteen men dressed in towels gathered around the fire. We removed jewelry and placed it in a pile outside the lodge. We filed in and sat in a circle around a big empty pit. I looked around and saw a beautiful frame of bleached branches above my head. Feathers hung from some of them. There was sage everywhere, and the aroma comforted me. The ceremony was about to begin.

Josh explained to me that this was a purification ceremony. There would be four sessions, or "doors." Each would last from fifteen to forty minutes. Large rocks that had been cooking in a fire pit all day would be brought into the lodge. They would be doused with sage water. We would offer prayers for the suffering, seek counsel from the group, and sweat together.

"If it gets too hot," he advised, "just put your face on the dirt floor. Sometimes it is a little cooler down there."

I lasted one and a half doors. It was just too hot. I couldn't breathe. I stood up in the middle of a sacred Indian prayer, tripped and stumbled my way around the circle, and dove out the door. I sat outside in the cool autumn air and waited for the ceremony to end. I felt ashamed, embarrassed, and disappointed. As I was preparing my apology for leaving, through the old carpet and ragged blankets I heard the leader ask the men to say a prayer for me and to honor my courage.

I had never heard anyone pray for me before.

My first impressions of the men at the sweat lodge—their few words, their silence—were very similar to my first impressions of Patches. I was to learn that it was the Indian way, that all relationships are sacred. Each is to be cultivated slowly and respectfully. It may be weeks before there is a smile, months before an embrace, years before trust. I cannot fault any Indian man for approaching me with caution. I cannot fault Patches for staying away. They share the wounds and heartache of too many betrayals and broken promises. There was only one woman at the shelter whom Patches respected and trusted. She happened to be part Cherokee.

So I began to watch instead of coax. In that silence, I learned about Patches. I saw the respect she commanded from every dog in the kennel, old and new. She was the matriarch, the Indian elder, the wise one. I never saw her whine and complain about her fate. When disturbed, she would retreat to the back of her kennel. There, she would sit tall and close her eyes as if to quiet the storms that raged inside her wild bones. Her eyes always spoke of the battle. The battle of two worlds—one of concrete walls, leashes, and chew toys and the other of prairie grasses, wild game, and dancing with the wind. Each day she faced it with dignity and grace.

It is the Indian way.

YELLOW DOG

....

I HAVE ALWAYS HAD A HARD TIME BEING ALONE. AS A child, I always went to sleep with the radio on. There was something soothing about hearing the voice of a disc jockey, hundreds of miles away in Cleveland or Pittsburgh, coming from a night table only inches from my ear. With Rusty at the end of my bed, the hall light on, and the crackling static of an AM radio by my side, the world didn't seem so big, the night so black. A little bit of light, a dog, and a radio—those were my perfect pals.

My dad always used to call me Pal. It made me feel warm inside.

Having a pal is different than having a friend. Perhaps it has something to do with an ease, a comfort. Friendships can be volatile, intense affairs. Pals never take themselves too seriously. Pals laugh at each other. And at life.

One of my best pals was named Yellow Dog.

He was wise and weathered, a salty dog who looked like he had spent a few too many nights in port drinking cheap whiskey and chasing the ladies. Yellow Dog had been found roaming the docks, abandoned by a sailor who decided he just wasn't going to take him out to sea anymore. He was a meat-and-potatoes kind of yellow Lab, rough around the edges and a little heavy around the middle. He had a weepy right eye and was graying up a bit around his big, happy mouth. His file said he was four. He and I knew he was pushing fifty.

A couple weeks after arriving at the animal center, Yellow Dog developed bloat, a very serious condition in which a dog's small intestine gets twisted. He survived a four-hour operation and spent a good part of his recovery resting on the soft carpeting in my office. During that time I fell in love with this grand old survivor.

We became best pals.

He loved to drink water. Gallons and gallons of water. And he would let everyone know how much he enjoyed it. He was the King of Slobber, the Sultan of

Slurp. Nothing made him happier than a fresh bowl of clean, cool water.

If I could only be content with such simple things.

As nature has it, if you consume a lot of water, you have to get rid of a lot of water. And from Yellow Dog's loins spilled the mighty Colorado. He would douse corners of buildings, inundate unsuspecting hedges, and flood small parking lots. He had a habit of wagging his tail when he relieved himself, and many times I found myself doing an impromptu jig to avoid getting soaked. Never was taking a dog outside to do its business such an adventure.

On one such walk, we ran into a rather stuffy Beverly Hills–type woman. She was pleasant enough but rather haughty, and when she asked me if Yellow Dog was "one of those dogs from the kennels," he looked up at me, casually lifted his leg, and peed on her Donna Karan silk slacks. She was horrified. I apologized for his unruly behavior and scolded him the best I could. She stormed away and we ran to the playfield together, laughing all the way. I'll never know whether I had waited too long to take him out or if he was just commenting on the woman's bad attitude. But I have my hunches.

Yellow Dog was one of the few dogs I have known who didn't have some kind of meltdown at the prospect of going for a ride in a car. I have had dogs jump into my lap while I'm switching lanes at sixty miles an hour. I have had dogs shed the equivalent of a full winter's coat on a trip to the deli. I have spent hours washing noseprints off windows and drool off consoles. The sight of a dog walking down the sidewalk on a leash has sent many of my dogs into a spinning, whining frenzy, usually while I'm trying to negotiate a busy intersection.

But Yellow Dog approached car trips in his usual easy manner. His lazy lope spoke of having seen it all. There were no big deals in his life.

He made this clear when I took him to a Jewish temple where I was to give a talk to some children about pet responsibility and care. Knowing that cleaning up after one's pet is a big part of responsible ownership, he decided to enhance my presentation by depositing five very neat piles of business by the *bimah* (similar to the Catholic altar).

The timing and placement couldn't have been worse. Or a point better made about the things dogs do.

I called a dear friend, who happened to be a member of the congregation, and told him what happened. He told me not to worry. He knew the rabbi was a witty and humorous man.

"He'll probably make Yellow Dog part of the Torah reading of the day," he joked.

I told Yellow Dog about my conversation. We both laughed.

Just like best pals do.

FRAZIER

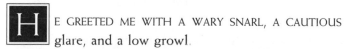

H E GREETED ME WITH A WARY SNARL, A CAUTIOUS glare, and a low growl.

Frazier frightened me. But for some reason, I didn't walk away.

I take an instant liking to certain people and situations. Others I approach with the same kind of wariness with which Frazier approached me. Either of those types of beginnings can grow into long and bountiful relationships. So I didn't try to force good nature upon him. I didn't rush to judge his reaction to me. I respected his need to give me a thorough going-over. After all, I was a very risky investment. His previous owners had walked away only hours before he and I met.

His skin was flaky dry, his fur lifeless. He was sickly thin—haunches too wiry, undernourished, and underloved. He was a street dog. "Perro de Calle," as they say in Tijuana. He was a chow/husky mix, a dicey combo to say the least. Chows were originally bred in China as palace guard dogs. Huskies like to pull sleds in subzero temperatures over great distances. It's not surprising that he didn't work out in that Pacific Beach condo.

In time he softened. Our courtship was awkward—an endless first date with lots of well-intentioned fumbling. When he finally started letting me into his kennel, he would leap up to greet me. I would yell "OFF!" push him away, turn around, trip on his blanket, and fall down. He would get excited again and jump up. I would yell "OFF!" and then find myself hugging him—half in desperation, half out of sheer love. He would playfully mouth my hand. I would yell "Nooo!!" and he would collapse in my lap. We would both laugh—I with lungs and throat, he with eyes and tail. Our relationship was not too dissimilar to a few of my first high school romances.

A couple months after Frazier arrived, he was diagnosed with kennel cough, a very infectious condition that can easily spread to other dogs. He was quarantined. I didn't see him for the better part of three weeks.

When he emerged some twenty-two days later, I could tell that something had changed. Can a prisoner thrown into solitary come out healthier and stronger? Can "time in the hole" ignite some kind of deep renewal?

What I saw was a different dog. His skin, beneath shiny fur, was pink and vibrant. A sparkle danced in his eyes. He was still rowdy and unpredictable, and he still disliked men who wore baseball caps and had beards, but he seemed to have recovered something in his solitude. If dogs can feel gratitude, I think Frazier had begun to feel some in the loneliness of that solitary kennel. Perhaps he had nothing else to compare his life with until he arrived at the center. A street dog knows the street. Nothing else.

Before I got my job teaching in Tijuana, I was unemployed for three months and forced to apply for food stamps. I had just turned forty. I was depressed and defiant, angry that I was in this position. In the waiting room of the welfare office I saw a young woman in a faded sundress juggling a wailing baby; men with ragged faces and thinning hair dragged deeply on cigarettes. It was a bewildered mass of broken dreams and wrong turns.

I remember thinking, "These poor, poor people. What a damn shame." And then I happened to look down at my own shoes. They were old and worn. My sweatpants were stained with coffee, no drawstring to hold them up. My T-shirt was torn at the shoulder. I hadn't shaved. My hair was a nest of greasy curls. I used to dress the same way when I was a highly paid fashion model in New York, but it was a fashion statement then. That morning I was not on assignment for *GQ*. I was applying for welfare, just like everyone else in the room.

In one moment (what a close friend refers to as an

"oh shit" moment), I saw my life as it really was. Not through the distorted lens of past success or future glory, but the way it was at that moment. I was officially disbarred from the "these things never happen to me" club. Yet I felt an immense sense of relief. For some reason, the anger disappeared. I didn't have to pretend anymore. There was a grand comfort in the knowledge that I was not alone. Until then, I had not realized how close I was to living on the street, and how fortunate I was compared with many of those who sat around me that morning.

Perhaps Frazier had a similar moment of clarity hearing the howls of a cellmate whose fate was much graver than temporary confinement. That particular dog, Solo, had been returned because of a biting incident. When a dog is designated as a "biter," it is virtually unadoptable because of the risks involved. It is extremely rare for a dog to be put down at the animal center, but biters face that fate. The fact that less than 1/2 of one percent of the thousands of dogs that come through the center each year are put to sleep never made those decisions any less agonizing for the staff. They were the darkest hours of the longest days.

When a dog is returned for biting, the other dogs seem to know. An eerie awareness settles over the kennel during those times. Frazier seemed to understand the consequences of such behavior, and he acted like a dog that knew he had been given a second chance.

And he got that chance. Two weeks after he had been released from quarantine, he was adopted. I was elated and astounded. However, even with his improvement, I had my doubts about his adoptability, mainly because of his constant struggle to control himself. He just overloaded too quickly.

Fifteen days later my fears were realized. Frazier was returned. He had become aggressive toward some children at a crowded public beach. Overloaded and afraid, he had tried to bite. The next morning, the decision was made to put Frazier to sleep.

I sat with Frazier the night before. He was his usual crazy self, excited by everything, unable to process all the information around him. We greeted each other with our signature assortment of cha-chas and scuffling, and we ended up tumbling to the floor together as usual. I sat on his tattered blue blanket. He brought me his ball and collapsed in my lap. He thrashed about like a beached tuna and paused for a moment to look at me. I held his head in my hands and stroked his chest. He began to wind down like a tired clock and for a few moments was still and peaceful. I cried and, like so many dogs in my life, he let me. I told him that it just wasn't going to work out this time, but that his heart was too big and good not to carry on in some way. It was all I could think of.

Perhaps it sounds foolish, but I know I will meet Frazier again someday. Maybe in the eyes of a silly puppy stumbling all over itself. In the determined gait of a street dog searching for food. Or in the howl of a newcomer behind a kennel door.

Frazier was put to sleep the next morning at 11:00. The kennels fell silent. It would be easy to say that it was just a coincidence.

But I know better than that.

The next day, my daughter called me from her grandmother's house in New York. She told me about a dream she had the night before about a dog and a blue blanket.

"Was it a scary dream?" I asked.

"No, Daddy," she replied. "It wasn't scary at all."

CANYON

....

WHEN I WAS A BOY, EVERY MORNING BEFORE SCHOOL my father made lunch for my brother and me. I can still see him standing in the kitchen in his pajamas, listening for baseball scores on the dusty radio that sat atop our refrigerator while he carefully assembled our sandwiches. Some days it was Virginia ham and Swiss cheese with mustard, other days roast beef with mayonnaise on a soft white roll. If we were really lucky, we'd unwrap our aluminum foil at school to discover last night's sirloin steak leftovers between two slices of Wonder bread with plenty of salt, pepper, and mayonnaise and a dash of Lea & Perrins. Each lunchtime held a tender mystery, and we were rarely disappointed.

Sometimes, hidden among the tiny red boxes of Sun-Maid raisins and plastic bags filled with vanilla wafers we'd find little notes or baseball scores. My dad knew that Roberto Clemente was my favorite player, so he always made sure I knew how many hits he had the night before.

"Three for Three" his little yellow note might say.

I have noticed that supermarkets offer an assortment of prefabricated lunches for children, packaged in bright and cheery boxes. They are perfectly neat, compact, and tidy. Convenient and easy. They contain anything from mini sandwiches, small squares of cheese, and tiny stacks of lunch meat to bite-size pieces of candy, brownies, and even miniature do-it-yourself cracker pizzas.

A few years back when I went in search of the perfect dog, I wanted one on the order of those prefab lunches—bright and cheery, neat, compact and tidy, convenient and easy. I didn't find one. In fact, I ended up with the exact opposite of what I was looking for—a big, goofy, fearful mess of a golden retriever named Canyon.

He is the dopiest, most uncoordinated wreck of an animal I have ever known.

After having lived with a very fearful and insecure dog for eleven years, I vowed that the next dog I got would be independent, sure, and strong. I thought I couldn't go wrong with a golden retriever.

"Overbreeding," my wife says.

Whatever the diagnosis, I am stuck with him. And

he is stuck with me. (If it turns out to be scientifically valid that dogs are the true reflections of their owners, I will immediately go into counseling. With three dogs, I probably should anyway.)

I got Canyon about a month after Squeeze died. I felt guilty looking so soon. I probably rushed into it too quickly.

I just got tired of missing her.

Canyon was the first dog that I looked at. The ad said: "Beautiful young male golden retriever. AKC, $40.00." My daughter and I went to see him.

He had been dumped in a side yard and ignored for the better part of his one and a half years. When his owner walked him to the front yard, it was as if Canyon was seeing the outside world for the first time.

A voice inside me said, "No! He's too much work! He's too much work!"

But I stayed and ventured in a little deeper.

These kinds of searches are affairs of the heart, and there seems to be a point of no turning back. Once I cross the boundary between caring and not caring, it's impossible for me to retreat to indifference. The moment I saw this terrified young dog, I felt a deep sense of responsibility and duty. It was clear that if I didn't take him, he would be returned to a place of loneliness, fear, and neglect. I couldn't walk away.

I decided to take him for a walk. He startled at almost everything—the rustle of a leaf in a tree, the slam of a car door. He almost leaped into my arms at the sight of a black garbage bag sitting in a driveway. He was like a newborn colt walking on a trail of rattlesnakes. I wondered whether he had ever left that side yard at all. I sat down on the curb and slowly pulled him over. My gentle pats and soft scratches echoed my daughter's promise.

"Don't worry, Canyon," she whispered. "We will take care of you."

We took him home. My wife was visibly disappointed. I couldn't blame her. He was a big project.

"We don't need any more big projects," she lamented.

For weeks, I tried to convince her.

"You know honey, he really is surprising me with his intelligence."

I kept trying.

"You know sweetheart, you may laugh, but beneath that dopey demeanor is a very smart dog. . . . And don't forget, he's registered AKC."

"American Knucklehead Club," she said.

I couldn't argue. He was a complete and total knucklehead.

Rarely have I seen a golden that could not gracefully retrieve a stick or catch a ball. I have ceased to play fetch with him for fear he may seriously injure himself. I have thrown balls five feet in the air and watched him land flat on his back. I have seen him confidently run twenty-five feet past a freshly thrown stick. A while back, he tried to turn around on a small walking bridge at a county park and fell off into the dry riverbed a few feet below.

We will not be hiking in the Grand Canyon anytime soon.

His tail is a lethal weapon when it comes to potted plants, Christmas ornaments, and cups of tea. Even small children are fair game.

He is reduced to convulsive fits and tremors at the sound of a leash. Trying to put a collar around his neck for a walk resembles a vaudeville routine. He'll sit for a second, jump up, sit down again because he knows it's wrong to jump up, then try to jump into his collar like a circus dog through a flaming hoop, miss completely, sit down again, shake, whine, tremble, belch, look at me, look at the door, look at me, look at the door, look at me.

Even the other dogs watch in disbelief.

Once I get his collar on, getting from the kitchen to the front door can be an adventure in and of itself. The combination of paws and toenails on a linoleum floor is very similar to the skating clowns segment at the Ice Capades. There is no talking sense or calm into him. I have tried to make him sit at the door, hoping he might be able to gather himself before we go out.

It's too painful to watch.

He looks like a chicken who can't stop laying eggs.

I have known a number of golden retrievers in my life and am fully aware of their hearty appetites and nondiscriminating palates. I have seen them devour turkey breasts and pumpkin pies set too close to the edges of countertops, swipe sticks of butter from dinner tables, and inhale kibble from cat dishes in a matter of seconds. My father's golden, Honey, was like a goat. She would eat anything. One of my most vivid memories as a teenager is of watching my father pull a pair of my mother's panty hose from Honey's backside one Saturday morning. Fortunately, Canyon has shown no interest in my wife's lingerie. He does, however, have a penchant for sweat socks, teddy bears, and small area rugs.

Like Squeeze, Brodie, and so many other dogs I have known, Canyon is most happy when chasing seagulls at the beach or galloping along trails in the forest. At these times, his true nature emerges. He sheds his clumsy ways, and many of his fears seem to evaporate into the skies. He becomes wise to the world around him—the air, the light, the earth. He is free. Free to do the things that dogs love to do.

It is a joy to behold.

When I first got Canyon, I was angry and disappointed with his behavior. I wanted him to be the perfect dog. But no matter what I said or did, he wouldn't change.

I tried to fix him. I read books. I sought counsel from friends. I listened to tapes in my car and rented videos. I took him to obedience class. Nothing worked.

Three months after I got him, I considered putting Canyon up for adoption. I was convinced that every dog on the other side of every fence was more obedient, better behaved, and less fearful than my own.

Then I started teaching at the animal center, where I met hundreds of dogs just like Canyon. Dogs who jumped up too much. Dogs who had too much energy. Dogs who barked too much. Dogs who were too much work. Dogs like Frazier and Champ and Cody. Orphans in a world filled with too many expectations and too little time. How close Canyon had come to being one of them.

Of all the lessons I learned during my time at the animal center, perhaps the greatest one is that imperfect dogs are no less worthy of love than are the so-called perfect ones. I had put this lesson into practice at the center but not in my relationship with my own dog. I suddenly realized it was time to stop searching for the perfect dog and start loving the one I had.

Tomorrow morning I will get up at about 6:30, walk bleary-eyed to the kitchen, and flick on the radio that sits atop the refrigerator. I will greet all the furry creatures gathered eagerly at my feet and maybe start some hot water for tea. I will yell for the first of many times to my daughter to get up as I begin to make her lunch. Peanut butter with a little marshmallow Fluff. I'll fill a Baggie with popcorn, cut up a kiwi, and wrap a piece of homemade corn bread in some foil.

"C'mon Hayden. . . . Time to get up!"

And when she opens her lunch at school that day, not just food will spill out on the table. A whole bunch of love will as well. If she's lucky, she might even find a Garfield cartoon.

As for Canyon, he will never be the dog who waits patiently in the back of my pickup while I sip coffee with a couple buddies at the local diner. He will never be a finalist in any Frisbee-catching contest. He will most likely not be the dog that sits obediently at my feet while I relax in my favorite chair reading the evening paper. He may never be the fearless, majestic, heroic dog of my dreams—the perfect dog.

But then, I will never be the perfect owner.

What a relief.

E P I L O G U E :
R U S T Y

....

T HERE HAD BEEN A NATURAL DRIFTING AWAY OVER
the years. By the fall of 1972, my after-school
wrestling matches with him in the front yard had long
since been replaced by my girlfriends, basketball games,
and college exams. Rusty was getting older, and so was I.

Like so many aspects of my childhood, my memories of his death are as fuzzy as those of his arrival. I
remember a phone call to my college dorm. I was home-
sick and lonely, and my mom and I hadn't been getting
along too well. I could barely hear her voice because of
the party going on next door.

"Gary," she said, "I have some bad news. Rusty died
this morning."

Someone knocked on my door and handed me a beer.

"Mom," I said, covering my ears, "it's kind of crazy here. Can I call you back?"

I hung up the phone and rested my head against the concrete wall.

It would be twenty-five years before I would cry the tears that filled my eyes that cold October night.

And on the eve of my forty-third birthday, I would call my mother to finish the conversation we had started so many years ago.

"Your father found him lying on the kitchen floor that morning," my mother recalled. "He couldn't get up. We called Dr. Barry and he told us to bring him over. It all happened so quickly. He had been fine the day before."

My throat felt dry as I picked up a photo that I kept on my desk—an eight-year-old boy hugging a perfect dog.

I began to remember the sound of his bark.

"Was he in a lot of pain?" I asked.

"If he was, he never let us know. Not a whine. Not a whimper. Your father took him up to the hospital. I couldn't go."

"I understand, Mom. Did you say good-bye?"

"Yes," she said. "Because when your father carried him down the front steps that morning, I had a feeling he wasn't coming back home."

I looked at the photo and thought of the many nights Rusty had slept on the end of my bed and kept my feet warm.

I began to remember the softness of his fur.

"I guess I never thought he would die," I said.

"I know," my mom said softly. "But when you left for college, I think he knew his job was finished."

"What job?"

As I put the photo back in its place, my mother replied, "Watching over you."